THE TENANT OF FIRE

To Robert,
Thank you for
supporting these poems
and for sharing the event
Ryan
3 Sept. NYC
2019

RYAN BLACK

WINNER OF THE AGNES LYNCH STARRETT POETRY PRIZE

Ryan Black

UNIVERSITY OF PITTSBURGH PRESS

Published by the University of Pittsburgh Press, Pittsburgh, Pa., 15260

ISBN 13: 978-0-8229-6590-9
ISBN 10: 0-8229-6590-9

Cover art: "Crooked Stair" Times Square Theater, NYC 1996 © Andrew Moore, courtesy Yancey Richardson Gallery
Cover design: Joel W. Coggins

THE TENANT OF FIRE

PITT POETRY SERIES *ED OCHESTER, EDITOR*

for my mother and in memory of my father

The mythic America is boyhood—

Leslie Fiedler

The devil wears a hypocrite shoe
The devil wears a hypocrite shoe
The devil wears a hypocrite shoe
And if you don't watch he'll slip it on you
There's no hiding place down here.

Traditional

CONTENTS

NOT ONCE

Listen:
    the early shadows whish an acclamation
born of steel threading steel for the Jamaica local,
its brake and stutter our only music. That,

and Olga Tañón, bootlegged, *Live from Mexico City.*
Or The Rolling Stones looped for three weeks in August
from the tenement's fourth floor,

from Bobby's apartment—*Some Girls.* Bobby, who even
in winter went about sleeveless displaying tracked arms
and once asked my first girlfriend

if he could taste her pussy, then threw all his furniture
out of the window. For years, he'd stop me at the turnstiles
and put his hand to my chest, his voice stunned

into pleasure. *It's so good,* he'd say, *don't even try it once,*
and to anyone who'd listen, *Please,* he'd say,
anyone at all, *not once.*
                        I want to believe that when Keats

began his famous ballad—his back to the low-burnt fire,
a heel slightly raised—when he wrote of the pale knight
and withered sedge, *La belle dame sans merci*

hath thee in thrall, it wasn't Spenser he considered. Can I say
Duessa was hardly on his mind, call Florimel an afterthought,
or even his brother Tom, buried at nineteen, that death

loitering through November? That it wasn't Fanny
who took the *kisses four,* or Poesy, but something closer
to our need to lose everything,

to try it once, then again and again until what? Bobby,
who would descend to the avenue and *nothing else*
see all day long as the steel frames of the overhead

dispersed midday light leaving streaks of blonde
across his curved back. Say what you will for industry,
it still delights.
                    If I could name it once, you'd understand.

HYPOCRITE SHOE

THE RISE OF THE COLORED EMPIRES

Those graves and our boulevard divide the morning light, and steer
      the new grass, the nimblewill and weed angling for life. Bereft of grief,
they mock maintenance with their stubborn shoots, a job I applied for, once,

      and didn't get. Instead, I was relieved of my boredom with a free pair
of Asics, three polo shirts, and the title "court attendant" at the U.S. Open.
      It was the summer the Williams sisters first flashed their brilliance

and an unseeded Russian was in love with the best hockey player
      on the planet. I was in love with no one. I read *Gatsby* for the first time,
and was alone in a way I'd never be again. From May until August, I worked

      the grounds crew, planting flower beds and spreading mulch beneath
a canopy of pine trees, preparing the park for CEOs, for two weeks
      of European money. It was easy work, and I was glad for it. At night,

I fell asleep with the light on, a book lying open, and, in the morning,
      rode the bus to Flushing Meadows, still wondering what Fitzgerald meant
by *the consoling proximity of millionaires*. I never found out. It didn't matter,

      really—I was out of high school, older than Venus, the same age
Serena would be when she'd raise her first singles title above her head,
      beating Amélie Mauresmo, the future world number one, in a third set

tiebreaker at the Open Gaz de France—but when I came to the scene
      where Tom Buchanan, through *The Rise of the Colored Empires*, lays
bare the nativist's science, an anxiety Fitzgerald certainly shared, I thought

      of my parents, and my parents' friends; I thought of their Friday night
card games, how my mother would extend the dining table with a leaf,
      and fill the refrigerator with cans of Budweiser, Baileys Irish Cream,

white wine, vodka, and cranberry juice. Then, she'd slice a fistful of celery,
      send me to the store for cigarettes. I loved the purpose. I loved the feel
of those bills in my hand, and the promise of enough change to buy

a quarter drink, orange or red. I'd pierce the top with a pin, sit quiet
on the landing as smoke filled the dining room, and the parents,
    all of them parents, would sit like sentinels in their chairs, griping

over fewer jobs, reduced hours, bad backs and bum knees. *Neighborhood's*
    changed, they'd say. *Tell me about it.* And I can see, now, the shape of habit
taking hold, so I'd like to stop here, to intervene on behalf of this moment

    before it hardens into verse, and is made grotesque. It's June, again;
the cherry blossoms burst beneath my window, a late blooming.
    At the French Open, Serena Williams is one match from winning

her sixteenth Grand Slam. She's favored, of course, but it's her power
    that's still praised, her brute strength, as if the game's impossible math
were divisible by broad shoulders and a snarl. She's set to face Sharapova.

    The city's split. *It is what it is,* Serena admitted. *At the French Open,*
the crowd boos, but they're young, they're kids, she added, thinking back
    to California, to 2001 at Indian Wells, where the sold-out crowd,

retirees and baby boomers, serenaded the sisters with worse than insult.
    Venus had withdrawn minutes before her semifinal match against Serena.
Two days later, at the finals, walking down with Venus to the players' box,

    Richard Williams turned to face the heckling crowd, nearly delighted
by the scene, grinned, and raised his left fist in the air like a wild John Carlos.
    Serena publicly thanked him. She's never returned to defend her title.

But Roland Garros is somewhere else; Paris a second home. Serena lives
    several months out of the year in a two-bedroom apartment off the Champ
de Mars. She bicycles the city, shops the open-air markets, her bookshelves

    lined with leather-bounds haggled over beside the Seine. Last summer,
she told John Jeremiah Sullivan that she comes here *to be around nobody,*
    to live alone, a part of the *Old World. It gave me the sense that she was*

hiding there, Sullivan would write, *hiding . . . from a country that couldn't decide*
if she was a goddess or a threat. And from her father, he added,
who years earlier promoted the girls as coming *Straight Outta Compton,*

a mythology sprung from the American century, because the work
of representation is the history it maps, rhetoric carried like torches
through the dark. Gatsby, for one, is never made to appear. He moves

through the narrative, *a fragment of lost words,* elusive, fading along
what Barbara Hill calls *the horizon of significance.* But it is only after
the *obscene word, scrawled . . . with a piece of brick,* is wiped clear

in the novel's final pages, a word Fitzgerald consciously omits: *kike,*
or *queer,* or something worse, a symbolic order of the hen-hearted and
dispossessed . . . It is only after Nick Carraway draws his *shoe raspingly*

along the stone, erasing the offense, that Gatsby can become a stand-in
for us all. And those card games, how there is no word for a displaced
fear, for disappointment still to come; how several of the players,

including my father, will not survive to contest this, so they sit here, mute
as the furniture, forever eyeing their no-good hands, delaying the inevitable,
caught in the instant before they can place their cards face down on the table,

and head to the kitchen for another drink.

THE BRIGADIER AND THE GOLF WIDOW

Pigeon-toed, a heartbeat like grace notes since childhood. Arthritic,
      widowed in her forties, the absence fostered like an avocation, making
her loneliness seem slight, though once, at the glad wedding of a niece,

      while the MC thinned the dance floor by anniversaries, *twenty years,* then *for*
then *sixty,* until one couple remained, in praise of fortunate nights, slowdancing
      through the high register of Lionel Richie's "Endless Love," my mother

left the indelicate hall in tears. Allergic to bee stings, to timothy grass
      and clover. Born among snowdrifts that cradled buses on Eastern Pkwy.
I've left a book of yours open on the nightstand for weeks now, a torn paperback,

      John Cheever's *The Brigadier and the Golf Widow.* I can't get through it.
I can't seem to read past the story—the one I'm supposed to love—
      of that feckless man who swims his way home, his route mapped by

Japanese lanterns, a riding ring. To be honest, most nights I read little else
      but your inscription, *Miriam Walsh,* the cleft peaks of that *M,* the glen
of your vowels, and the *s* asleep in the shade of telephone poles. *Miriam,*

      from the Hebrew meaning "bitter," meaning a plight, and the namesake
who sang freedom out of Egypt, chosen by your mother, though your father
      would balk at the denotation. *Walsh,* meaning "native," from the Irish meanir

"foreigner." *60 Autumn Ave.* I think of the assonance in that address, of how far
      you must have felt, at nineteen, from the midday parties of Westchester.
Or Connecticut. Or wherever Bullet Park. Or I think of Mary Walsh,

      variant on *Miriam,* your girlhood friend, struck and killed outside
The Crow's Nest in 1967. Her mass card's still tucked into the mirror
      of your vanity. And beneath it, a black and white photograph, you and Mary

at the bow of a Stier house on Euclid Avenue. Mary's beaming like a film still.
      Skirt suit and cloche, white gloves. I know so little about her; I've never aske
But you, you're off-center; you're looking past the camera, as if prescient,

as if you meant to leave. *Miriam Walsh*, bitterness, native and foreigner.
In the fifth grade I was pulled from class by Sister Rosalita. My grandfather
        died six months prior, and my grandmother, alone for the first time in 53 years,

sold the house, *60 Autumn Ave, B'klyn 8*, and started hearing voices. *Sundowning,*
        the doctors named it, *early dementia*. Innocent, at first: an overstocked
refrigerator, *my daughter needs baking soda*. Then, the unthinkable,

        my daughter's been killed in a car accident, tell the boys. So when
the Sister of Charity took my hand, and knelt as if beside a pew,
        an awkward reverence I'd come to resent, I knew enough to keep

my mouth shut. The dim hallway, the tableaux of hand-traced turkeys,
        of Indians and pilgrims on popsicle sticks. But what I think back on,
what I see best is the covenant, the papier-mâché feast that ballooned

        from the wall like an accordion. *How strange and fine to get so near to it,*
to touch the hem of her habit, to lose something once, then retrieve it
        in the telling. My mother was fine, for sure, I was certain. My mother,

Miriam Black, her loss irretrievable, her name elegiac, "to pass undetected,"
        again and again, who left her niece's wedding in shame. For years after,
she'd visit her mother at Rockaway Park, Beach 115. Each visit the same:

        my grandmother, lost in the discord of her memory, impossibly thin,
would ask for my father, gone five years, gone ten. *How's Jimmy?*
        she'd ask, and my mother, without fail, each time would answer,

He's fine, Mom. He's on his way.

THIS IS CINERAMA

Because the foot fractures, because the body turns soft. Because
    the mind says *six miles nine miles twelve miles,* and I haven't run
in weeks. Because another relationship is ended, I take two Advil,

    and go to the movies. A retrospective; the sixtieth anniversary print
of *This Is Cinerama,* Lowell Thomas's love note to technology
    and travel. It opens with Thomas, in black and white, behind a desk

littered with paper, lecturing on a history of representation. Cave
    drawings, Egyptian murals, the Renaissance on the verge of motion.
Then motion: Kircher's magic lantern and the zoetrope, Mathew Brady,

    father of photojournalism, bringing his studio to the battlefields
of the American Civil War. By the time Edison enters the narrative,
    Lowell Thomas has turned reverent. The Black Maria, the penny arcade.

Valentino and Banky. Then, *Ladies and Gentlemen,* he intones, sounding
    every bit the showman he'd become, *This Is Cinerama,* and the curtain
opens, revealing a louvered screen curved in ratio to the retina.

    It's 1952. Rockaway Beach. To demonstrate the full scope of their vision,
the filmmakers have rigged their tri-lens camera to the front car
    of the Atom Smasher, the wooden roller coaster at Rockaways' Playland.

I walked its ruins as a boy; a housing complex, now. A shopping center.
    But, tonight, its motored gears clack and catch as we climb the lift hill
to a pan vista of the Atlantic shoreline, then drop like a bucket

    into the first banked turn. The audience howls; they throw their arms
into the air. The images are dizzying. The man beside me records
    the sequence on his cell phone. But the tone shifts by a long dissolve,

and we're taken to Milan, to La Scala and the Temple of Vulcan.
    It's the first-act finale of Verdi's tragic opera, the grand set piece where
Radamès and Aida will later be entombed. The camera's static, mournful.

Culture, thought Thomas. *Spectacle and sound.* And from there,
the scale just grows: Niagara Falls, "A Mighty Fortress Is Our God,"
sung by the Long Island Choral Society. Spectacle and sound. The tour

of Europe, the Basilica San Marco, monuments to fallen empire,
though somewhere between the Schönbrunn Palace and Zaragoza's
Plaza de Toros, I lose interest, my mind wanders. I think of you.

Of your mother's dying. How I heard it from a friend, who spoke plainly,
as if discerning the weather. We'd been out of touch, you and I,
for more than a year, but I wanted to find you, then. To go to you.

To say something to a life without her. I wished I'd been there when
you learned; a stranger to your grief. I was still a boy when my father
died. Foreign to me, now, that loss was absolute, unadorned. And so,

it was manageable. I cried in spasms until I slept. A vexed relationship
persists, I think. Nothing cools. When the movie ends, I sit slumped
in my seat until the lights come back, until an usher eyes me from

across the theater. I want to show someone how they got it wrong.
You missed the point; you got it wrong. But I've been telling stories,
again. I've been talking to myself. The truth is: I haven't been

to the doctor. My foot swells, but I haven't seen a doctor. The truth is:
the film was screened *last* summer, at the Cinerama Dome in L.A.
And because the sun in California is the sun in California, because

New York is out of sorts. Because another relationship is ended,
I can think of nowhere else, no one else but you. We walked North Beach,
talking about adaptations, about Flushing Meadows, La Flor Bakery,

about your mother, who was gone, and, what more, I can't remember.
We said goodbye at Fourth and King, and the waning light made your face
look younger. And knowing. Later, I followed the basin to AT&T Park,

bought a ticket from a scalper, in the left-field bleachers. There was no

moment of her going, nothing to call back or contend. *You can't spend what you ain't got,* the song goes. *Can't lose what you never had.* I tried

calling in the seventh, but you didn't answer. The Giants tied it in the ninth, then won it on a walk-off.

HOME BY THE SEA

I can't turn around and put up a flag and say, "I have no place to go."

Chief Dennis Diggins
Bureau of Waste Disposal, DSNY

From bridge view, from snow-packed
rock. Seagirt to West End. The crude

signs nailed to garage doors, inked
on windshields, *Looters will be crucified.*

November: an Old World threat. A FEMA
truck stutters by on a busted axle. Drywall,

plumbing, dining set, bureau. Nine days
passed. At Fitzgerald Gym, two mothers

braid their children's hair with Vaseline.
On state-issued cots below the free

throw line.

SKIP TO MY LOU

Junior hustles near The Showboat
playing Bitch for sneakers.

He's got a handle, can go left or right,
through you or over you. They call him

Man-Child or Sweet Sweet-Jesus or
Skip-to-My-Lou because he stands upright

and skips down the court daring you
to reach. When his daughter needs milk,

Junior plays for dollars. He's got eyes
like wet cement. Sticking Junior is like

finding your name in a graveyard.

COMPENSATION

The Queens 11 idles on Metropolitan,
coughing like a life-long smoker
and clogging the gate to Saint John
Cemetery, diocese of Brooklyn, as Hector
speeds through the crosswalk, last
in our procession. A traffic camera
flashes in his rearview, tripped, clear
as a floodlight. Knights of Columbus,
forgive us these hand-me-downs,
our fathers' suits, ill-fitting and frayed;
pardon a burnt-out spark plug, the $50
citation; we've no business burying
the dead. *Fuck me,* Hector shouts,
pounding the dashboard. His button-down
is cuffed above the wrist, his hair close
cropped. *Fuck you, too.*
                         Emerson believed
that when a man dies young, he dies into
the angels of our derivation, and that we,
in this world, are compensated, made
new by the loss. A year after losing
his first wife, a year of terrible imaginings,
Emerson returned to the grave, cooled
by her last words, *I have not forgot the
peace and joy,* and opened the coffin's lid—
lay always before me, even in sleep.

Frankie died in a hospital bed, sedated,
the same age as Keats. The flawed cells
slowed, at first, then spread as if spilled,
as if decreed, blossoming markers
in the bloodstream. Hector suspended
his life like a lover. I visited once.
With Giuseppe. Later, I sat at my desk,
marking my grief like a sermon. Tone

and texture. Image. Exposition. We must
insist the dead knew our love, that they
risked joy, above all, and were not afraid.
Frankie was asleep when we arrived,
his brother waved us in. *Dennis just
left,* he said. *Go ahead. Sit.*

                    Once,
at the Bridge Bar, drunk and intractable,
Frankie bet $20 he could swim Jamaica
Bay, then slid beneath the back deck,
and disappeared into the dark water to
turn up, four hours later, at the Dunkin'
Donuts on Rockaway, soaked to the bone.
But picture the high school sophomore
working the only register, singing *ready
or not, here I come, you can't hide,* and
her bright voice, then Frankie coming in.
Can you see the look that must have held
her face as she punched up *small coffee,
croissant,* and Frankie, now shirtless,
shuffling his feet as the late night A,
outside, moves by? Headlights move by,
mornings and weekends until the plastic
letters of the Crossbay marquee fade
and fall off. But it wasn't that way. Time
doesn't work that way; it couldn't have.
Time's common; it wades like a swimmer
through black water, exhausted, certain
of nothing but a stubborn will, hands
parting the filthy bay, a sneaker kicked
off and sunk to car parts and glass.

AT BROAD CHANNEL

The dry reeds, deep left field, bend basin-ward in the constant thrum
　　　of Kennedy International. Wasps whirl above rims of Pepsi cans left,
between innings, on a rotting bench as the coach examines his boys,

　　　bends their ears back and combs through their hair, *any bare skin . . .*
tuck your pants into your socks. And, later, in the fine light from plastic
　　　lamps, in a rented studio facing the boulevard, the sound of those flights

still in his ear until he imagines nothing else, nothing but music
　　　in the arrival and departure of strangers, he'll hold a mirror to his chest
and part the hair with a tweezer. There are times when he can almost feel

　　　what isn't there, or what might be, the mind's sleight-of-hand, and because
he wouldn't know where to look next, let me start again. I was in love
　　　with a woman I thought I could leave. In the end, of course, she left me.

And left for good. And what I felt then isn't shame, or what I've learned
　　　shame could be, but my whole body ached. *Without reason,* the doctors said.
It just ached. So I imagined a disease still overlooked, a thief in the bloodstream,

　　　and I'm thinking of Polly Murray, of Lyme, Connecticut, 1955. I'm thinking
of her first headache, sore throat and fever, the periorbital rash and bleeding.
　　　And I'm thinking this is about resentment, the doctors' response, *syphilis*

perhaps, perhaps lupus, and who could blame her, ferried from the sick
　　　to the troubled by an expert's sloppy font. *Fish handler's, German measles.*
But it must have been indifference that stayed her, those sweet hours

　　　when she'd strip before the river and wade out into the current, alone,
the jeweled stars blinking. Or early mornings in bed with her husband,
　　　how they'd fuck in silence as the children slept far beyond Lyme, and far

beyond their own bodies, if only for an instant. Thirty years to get it all
　　　down, to separate and divorce. Thirty years to help give name to the disease
poised to bloom across the pale chest of this shortstop, playing in on the grass,

who spits now into the palm of his glove, a prayer the ball does not find him
but a moment, as well, his body can record in its brief and almost grace.
Soon his eyes could blur, his fingers swell. Soon the simplest geometry

might set him off, and his knees will burn. Or the soft voice of his heart
might stutter and spit, prophesying a long convalescence, the get-well-cards
addressed out-of-state. Then the body's dominion. Or he'll return by spring,

somehow quieter, somehow new, giving up soda and chocolate, *for Lent*,
he'll say, though the fine muscles shine past any faith. And who wouldn't
want it this way? Who doesn't wish it so? But I remember a boy in eighth

grade who lost an ear on the Interboro when his brother's Nissan flipped
at Cypress Hills, the same fool's turn we'd soon race through to excite our
first girlfriends. He was pinned, I think, in profile to the open sunroof;

his ear caught, shaved. And if we made fun of him then, if someone
who has long since forgotten first called him Vincent, and he was made
to carry that name into a strange adulthood the way the young artist carried

his stillborn brother like a pall in that famous signature, we must have been
afraid. I think we must have been terrified. And if the body's the form of
prayer and all we believe tethered to it, what then? And the woman

from Lyme? Or the one who left? Ask the moon. Ask the darker half
of twilight. Or the boys soft tossing between starts of a doubleheader,
spraying Repel onto their cleats and forearms, and replaying the first

inning error or pair of strikeouts, the dropped fly ball and hit-by-pitch?
There is no voice in the wind here, no truth in the stalled parkways the wind
moves through, and the boy who lost an ear somewhere in this poem

must be a man by now, though some things will not change, some things
are absolute, like a truth spoken for the first time, and I can imagine
him this evening, a look like wonder etched into his face as he stares

again at his own reflection. It's already late; the last planes pulse and
broadcast home. And I'm sorry for knowing this, but, each time, nothing
happens. He stares, and nothing happens. And, each time, he can almost

see what isn't there, what's indivisible: a tick on a blade of grass, the body
in negative space.

AT STEEPLETOP

And van Gogh in Arles, impatient for Gauguin, argues the price of a mirror
      to work again from his own image because, *at present,* he writes, *the élan*
of my body is such that goes straight for its goal. Bas-relief, quarry and till,

      the parsonage, the Borinage, *Scenes from Clerical Life,* St. Rémy still to come.
It's June in the Taconic Hills, storm clouds and a low fog and you in California
      where it never rains, Minneapolis long between us. I'm reading piecemeal

from the selected letters of Vincent van Gogh, in a converted barn bought from
      a Sears & Roebuck catalog. At Steepletop. I know it's in bad taste to write poem
about a residency, but this isn't a poem, is it? It's a taunt, a love letter.

      A status update you'll spy in the newsfeed. A sheathed cupid guards the conc
pool, neglected now, where Millay insisted her guests swim nude as she watched
      from a spare room to choose her next lover. Thyme overgrows the tennis cour

our playwright adds it to the soup. But there's a story here the caretaker loves
      to tell, of the first elephant brought to the U.S., and after a tour of the farmhou
of Millay's library and parlor, the modern kitchen remodeled by *Ladies' Home*

      Journal, the "withdrawing room" with its twin pianos where Eugen had scratch
out an eye from the bust of Sappho; after narrating Millay's death, miming the fall
      from the top of the staircase, the wineglass and snapped neck, the unfinished

manuscript left on her desktop, the caretaker will tell you of Old Bet. *It happened*
      here, he'll say. *On East Hill Road. The first elephant in the U.S.* And you'll know
right off what you're hearing is myth. An elephant suffers in Orwell's prose

      to give his metaphor consequence, but Bet dies like an engine. She shudders o
then stops. Without a name, an elephant is unimaginable, so the illiterate farmer
      shot her as she passed his fence line. And the caretaker will insist George Bail

bought her from a sea captain, who picked her up in London a few weeks prior.
      She was fifteen years old, more than 6,000 pounds, and upwards of eight feet high,
but the description is patched from the Essex Register, and attributed

to Benjamin Lent. I heard the rest at Yellow House Books, from Bonnie Benson,
herself a Bailey. *Old Bet was killed,* she said, *but in Maine, not Austerlitz. Far*
from Steepletop. And not out of fear, she added, *but for the sins of the poor.*

She sold me a signed copy of *Winter Stars.* By 1941, stricken and strange,
Millay rarely left the bedroom. She began charting her drug use: *3/8 gr. morphine,*
self-administered. Cigarettes (Egyptian). Beer & martini. Demerol. Benzedrine.

One night, she asked to see Joseph Freeman alone in her study. They hadn't
spoken in years. Millay, self-pitying, *pale and fragile,* asked him to read some
new poems, then, pleased at his reaction, she took his hand and kissed him.

Not the kiss of Eros, he'd write, a decade later, still convincing himself, *the kiss*
of Agapé; warm, loving, and chaste. The lie we chose was plain and complete;
that I could imagine you as a child pumping your legs on a swing set in Pusan;

that you could stare at a kettle pond and see the ball fields that flooded in summer;
that it mattered somehow, if only to us. Tonight, I'm thinking only of you.
And I'm sorry for so little, it's startling. But what if everything left between us

were a difficult pleasure, without recompense? I stole a bottle this morning
from Millay's vanity, a postscript to her late addiction. I don't know why
I should tell you this. I doubt I'll put it back.

WHEN THE WORLD'S ON FIRE

My name is the merciless Old World.
Juan Baptista. I took my son at nineteen

months, I've known his life without me:
July, the Crown Motor Inn. I hooped

a cord around his neck and hanged him
from a curtain rod, then held his weight

beside the tub, a shallow of bone. Thin
relic. His mother, she'll wear white;

her brothers, my sister. And I'll burn for
what I've seen. They've no providence

left to keep him in.

ON THE COOLING BOARD

Your logic can be overtaken by your sense as a parent.

Michele James

New York Newsday, Sept. 2, 1985

Cardboard cut to mean a grave; pall
and procession, the boy holds his breath

like a seal. *Keep still,* she says—his mother—
a prompt. He throws his leg over the makeshift

box, shuts his eyes. Greasepaint, talc. Rubberneck,
and their doubt's laid bare: *Save Our Kids,*

Keep AIDS Out. South Ozone Park, P. S. 63.
Not the faith-stung or poor, but a disheartened

class. Placards spy the walkways. Lucky one,
keep still. Your likeness is enough

to fool this world.

VICTORY FIELD

WHY BOTHER?

Because even in the deep neighborhoods of Queens, Jonathan Franzen
        can find a houndshark, the smooth dogfish splayed beneath the bench
of an N train, rotting out, promising an empty car on a Wednesday night

        in August, the worst heat of the summer, though some will mind an awful
smell to pose the dead with props—a cigarette, a MetroCard, an open can
        of Red Bull—the images posted to Instagram before a transit officer

can carry the shark out in a garbage bag. But, Jonathan, this isn't figurative.
        The dead dogfish is not a metaphor for the end of the social novel. And on
streets where Hindi, Russian, Korean, and Colombian Spanish, by which

        you must mean Jackson Heights, *are spoken in equal measure,* though
you'll cut *Colombian* in revision, even here where in 1991 *ugly news*
        could still reach you, no one speaks the dark and vegetating language

of shark. Why bother? Because the first word my niece spoke with proficiency
        was goodbye. *Goodbye, park. Bye-bye, trees. Goodbye, Uncle Ryan.*
There, there now. *Goodbye.* I'd read on trains that stitched the borough like a syntax

        how an elegist submits to the ineffectual, that language is *an equation*
of the dissimilar, undone as easily as Penelope's loom. *Gone,* we say,
        and ask something of permanence, an exchange, but the elegist,

inheriting a chorus, sings in half-forgotten grief, and the dead are made to rise
        from the churchyard of poems to a votive of April stars. *Goodbye, Mommy.*
Goodbye, Da-da. Think of my sister, collapsed at the foot of her bed, an artery

        hemorrhaging in the frontal lobe of her brain. Think of the EMT who radioed
overdose to Queens East, *cardiac dysrhythmia,* then held my sister's head
        to the side to draw out vomit with a gloved hand. At the hospital, it took

three men to sedate her, her body decoding each signal as threat, and when
        her husband called there was no news—no planned surgery, no tomograph—
so he repeated her name for its simple truth, like an apostrophe, or like a child

learning their way into the new world. Six years from holding his only daugh
And if grief's a republic of worthless currency, make it prose, just once. Give it
consequence. Or let him be lonely.

VIA NEGATIVA

Advancing in pairs, sun-washed, and ducking imagined artillery, we closed
        on the cinder track, a French shore transposed and fortified with hockey
sticks and wifflebats borrowed from Miss Reid's gym bag, Field Day

        for the newly confirmed of Saint Thomas Apostle, men in the eyes of God.
Peter mocked German as we drew near, grunting consonants and nonsense,
        and laughing. And Alberto crouched in fake pain, the son of corner-store

jewelers, pale-skinned as though already dead, a silver cross glinting at his neck,
        shouting, *Remember the Alamo,* before shutting his eyes and dying. At twelve,
we had no language for this but *Omaha, Utah,* cities of salt and corn stalks,

        the lessons taught by Miss Pica, who smoked on the bleachers as we played
war beside Victory Field blond in the sun. Then Sarah pointed at what she
        imagined was a company of horses on the soccer fields, and ran to them.

I remember a woman in summer, her voice alone carrying from the tenement
        across my window, guttural and screaming, though my father would only say
she dreamed in a dead language. So I dreamed of a woman mouthless,

        her fingers held where her lips should be and eyes widening in that deformed
silence. Imagine every word you spoke were a valediction, that to order fried eggs
        with coffee and buttered toast is to admit a possible end. And just how desperate

you really are. Now imagine yourself as a child, nine perhaps. You're listening
        to this woman and, finally, it's *murderers* she screams, and you're thankful
for it; you're almost calmed. But now she doesn't stop. *Murderers,* she screams,

        again and again, until you turn to the cross nailed to your wall and ask Him
to come down. *Son of God, three days from salvation, thorns forever drawing*
        the same blood, come down. Come down as He had for Miss Pica when

she followed His voice into traffic, or so the story goes, and was lifted above
        trucks and compacts like the blessing of the body, and softly placed, in broad
daylight, on the corner of Woodhaven and Jamaica, the spectacular path of faith.

Come down as He had for Alberto when a stray bullet pierced his temple
and cleaved to skull, cradling between membrane and marrow, and stunning
    the doctors who chose, finally, to leave it be, doing little more than guesswork

little less than prayer. Come down as He had for Joseph in his shame,
    or Bartimaeus blind, *faith made thee whole.* Come down for this woman who
continues to accuse the summer and the night of the unthinkable. I'm sure, now,

    she must have called out, as well, to the bare oaks in winter, but I was years
from learning our role in the war, of *Omaha, Utah,* and further still from hers,
    so I clung to a word despite its abstractions and dismissed the rest as strange.

But think of that language she dreamed in, extinct, made meaningless. And picture
    my mother, how she slept, still as any landscape, and moonlight spilling over
the floorboards in pools of light, and my father's chest, how it rose and fell

    like the bow of a delicate ship ten miles offshore. We learn to ask of what
we can, or never learn at all. We say, *There is no God and Mary is His mother,*
    but, once, in seventh grade, a dove white as a blizzard landed on the open sill

as Miss Pica divided the board into *Allied, Axis,* and *Occupied.* And struck by
    what could only be the hand of God, the true vision of Christ, she collapsed
behind her desk, sending the dove from its perch above the rectory and over

    a pewter statue of Saint Thomas.

THE LEMON ICE KING

Forest Park's band shell opens from a slumped arc,
weatherworn and whale gray, that at this hour,
if you stare long enough, starts to fall, topple over,
then quickly rights itself as if nodding off
and waking. The autumn sun seeps from oaks
and cedar beeches, pouring over the steering column
of a stripped car. Come winter, we'll drag its hood
up the thin hills of the nine-hole public course
along with trash lids, milk crates, shopping carts,
the plexiglass from bus stops and, once, a bookcase
Peter and I found on Atlantic, the shelves warped
and splitting. It was late in the season;
the slopes had all but iced. Peter leaned forward
gripping the legs, urging us ahead,
the cold wind burning my ears,
and the bookcase shuddering its descent
until we hit a mound of solid snow
and split in two.
                    That winter, the forecast was general:
snow over the stalled parkways beside Creedmoor
glazed with ice, snowfall hitting Jamaica Bay
and breaking in its dark water,
snow and sleet pelting Queensbridge.
LaGuardia delayed, Kennedy rerouted.
Our borough turned white as the park carousel's
lone Andalusian, pride of D.C. Muller, modeled
from Napoleon's forgotten Spanish bounty—
undiluted, pure.
                    When the season turned,
the city hired Junior to touch up the crests, hocks,
hindquarters and fetlocks, cantles and saddle flaps
of the carousel herd, but we knew him from the murals
he painted on our handball courts—maps of Colombia
and his daughter's birth date, an interlocking NY,

cityscapes, and a larger-than-life portrait
of Alejandro Sosa, Pacino's cocaine supplier
in *Scarface.*

      One summer, for The World Cup,
The Lemon Ice King paid Junior eighty dollars
to cover its walls with the flags of quarterfinalists,
then paint over the eliminated after each round.
Spain lost in regulation, the U.S. screened
by primer, then Sweden and Bulgaria,
until the Italians on Myrtle closed early,
placed their faith in Baggio's sore right ankle
only to watch Romário slice the net and collapse
into a flag that replicates the Brazilian night sky.

Corona erupted. Elmhurst, Jackson Heights.
Car horns blared Queens Boulevard and the avenues
of this their home—borough of airports
and parkland, of Robert Moses lost in the ghosts of brake lights,
Lefrak City, The Lemon Ice King, an asylum
whose patients look down through barred windows
at the Grand Central and call it a river.

STAGGER LEE

*Surely, they cannot be deluded
as to imagine that their crimes
are original?*

James Baldwin
"Staggerlee Wonders"

Tree limbs stripped by slow degree,
the blunt edge of a busted rake.

Box cutter, boot heel. *If Stagger Lee's
on the boulevard,* raised hand and

kinked fist, *oh cruel Stagger Lee.*
Howard Beach of Bergin Hunt

and Fish Club, of Fourth of July's
Kiddie Kastle moonwalk: December,

the gap in a chain link fence, a dead end.
Michael Griffith, born into the path

of that old, sweet chariot.

OMMIE WISE

In underbrush, half-buried, a suitcase.
Teeth marks. Plea deal.

We'd pinned fliers to telephone poles,
height and hair color. Nobody

is ever missing. March, the Queens
County Morgue, and the body

disarticulate. Split bone, spine.
Newark to 88th Road, and Edwin

stammering defense: *I'd sooner mm-
meet the devil th-than be that*

woman's man.

THE CONJURER

If there's a place the mind can hide, it's in the thick coat of the Bengal tiger
    glimpsed beside the Interboro, white as the first touch of frost in the almond
blossom. A thing like that, well, you keep your distance. You learn to hold still.

    So the men who showed, at first, would only kneel, their guns drawn and fixed
on what they'd later call *beautiful,* escaped, it turns out, from the temporary
    camp of the New Cole Bros. Circus, not by picked locks or from challenge

cuffs, but her handler's absent craft. *Baby's breath. Infinite.* And I heard
    management wanted her sold, or else forgotten, their only draw no longer
worth the cost. Diminishing returns, I guess. Insurance and transfer. But then

    they hired locals to sweep the grounds, hose down the cages and paint the booths,
men who'd work for very little. Which meant between nods, or half-drunk. Or dusties
    lacing PCP with whatever they can. If I say embalming fluid, you'll cringe, turn

away. Parsley, and you'll blush. And I'll know my luck is sung, that the white
    tiger still cleans her paw in a trailer bound for Syracuse, where she'll sleep
until noon beneath a roof of painted-on stars. Desire is that permanent, etched

    into the body the way the body remembers salt, how muscle remembers work.
But there's an end to the imagination's reach, a place where the mind can only
    hide, and you meant to tell me of your father's stroke, of precision and cross-

stitching, the rheumatic fever, Sparmannia, sparrow. It's the first warm night
    in April, and your shoulders are bare. You've taken off your shoes, curled
your toes in the new grass. *Six years,* you'll say, *and two months,* and I'll

    tell by your voice, almost querulous, the sure sprain of wonder. *How strange
and fine to get so near to it,* you'd say if someone hadn't already. In Australia,
    Houdini, vaudeville conjurer, con man and sometime medium, stood at the edge

of The Queens Bridge, weighted with chains, the Yarra sloshing its metaphor
    against the stern of twin rowboats, and listened. *For the voice,* he once told
Lady Doyle. *It comes as easy as stepping off a log, but you have to wait*

for the voice. So the stage was set and, this time, the great conjurer's buried
his trick in a boot's tongue. Curtained by the river, he frees his hands first, then
        works his legs, dislodging a corpse in the thrashing, which rises to the expect

crowd, gooseskinned, distended. And I can't help but read this as directive,
        that the illusion made real is somehow the point, the comedy told in reverse
Too close, Houdini must have thought as he climbed the wharf, cast irons glinting

        in his raised left hand. Growing up, I had a friend whose mother worked nigl
at Jamaica Hospital. When her husband left them, she took on extra shifts
        and fell into the habit of collecting photographs from the emergency room,

clipped and arranged on her dining table, displayed with the same care
        a conjurer's assistant must showcase her wardrobe. We took notice, of course
but she never said a word about them. And though it is wrong to guess anything,

        I think she, too, meant to instruct, to steer us somewhere near the ineffable,
or the how and when of not getting it right. Tonight, my father's been gone
        twelve years. And your father's still sick. But I meant to tell you

of the Bengal tiger, how she hurt no one and simply walked through the picnic
        of a Berean missionary choir, their gathered breath, their hosannas and awe.
I wanted to say how she came to the Interboro, immaculate, flooded in light,

        and stopped there as though hitting her mark, half-a-mile from the grave whe
Houdini's body was blessed, grieved, and buried, where it's almost believed,
        if you listen close enough, you can even hear the dead.

AN OFFERING OF STEAM

She pulls closed the screen door
to her backyard half-shaded now
by tenements, and turns on the sink.
Her hands ache as though they've pulled
a thousand roots of wildflowers:
loosestrife and milkweed,
black-eyed Susan, cinquefoil.
Dirt pocks her neck and forehead,
and darkens the skin beneath her nails—
a row of earth she tends,
shaped by cement, long after the city
ordered its lone tree cut; the trunk
infested and hollowed by beetles,
branches snapping
in soft wind.
          Four years have passed
since her husband felt something honed move
through his chest and, not knowing its strength,
shut his eyes—something she carries now
like a stone in heart.
Loosestrife, she says. *Milkweed*,
her voice hushed, frayed.
            Last spring,
her youngest son moved west over
wheat fields, past silos and sandstone cliffs,
to a city cast from ice. And sometimes,
at night when he calls, she hears
in his voice the still, blunt music
of that unbearable heart.
She turns on the hot water as snow
melts around him running plainly
at the street's edge—this woman,
alone in her kitchen, reciting
the names for weeds
as steam floods the sink

and lifts through her hands an offering,
and softens her skin and nails,
and softens as it rises
to the plastered ceiling.

IN THE PINES

I always knew the house was on fire. It was one of the first things I knew.

Alice Notley

Shiver for me now—the road through
the park, the scum kettle pond,

the planned pine grove past Victory
Field, and the block where she

burned last night. March, a cracked
cellar door, *don't you lie to me.*

Cuffed wrists. Duct tape. I am
a luckless thing. A man's

rended heart. I burned like brush
fire in the pines. Burned

like the front porch.

MOTHERLESS CHILDREN

Born deaf, fork-tongued. Born in salt
marsh at Flushing Bay. South Jamaica.

With night sweats. Born from flotsam
and broom wire; in a hard time, I don't

owe you a day. From power lines at
Ravenswood that lit Queensbridge like

a plaza, like Skip-To-My-Lou, my civic
drum. Uncounted, *one of the roughs.*

In a Willets Point chop shop, *a kosmos.*
It cost everything to sing this, now watch

me give it away.

4-A

1.

And the thin grief called sincerity is born, the city that never was
called to order so that even the absent bride has her say, in a bathroom
stall at Blessed Sacrament, her veil tucked into a handbag and creasing.

But it's not what you think; cold feet don't hold her. And our groom?
Our groom is sure as gospel. Still, she waits, her hair a loose sweep
pinned behind the ear, her dress slip-stitched and buttressed beneath

a frill, and she pauses now not for her sake, and not for a moment's
doubt, but in the missteps of a manuscript, because the story begins
before their vows, in East New York before a war, on a pitcher's mound

in Highland Park beside Cypress Pool and a cemetery for the Union
dead. The pitcher's a southpaw, still in high school. His uniform
collects at the hip like an empty rucksack as he leans into the stretch,

shakes off a sign, and comes to the set checking back the runner, only
to hold the ball awhile longer in the shield of his glove, then step off,
toe the rubber, and start again. Even style has a habit of confessing.

Think Preacher Roe, one scout noted, *with Johnny Podres's changeup,*
but today it's the slider stinging the mitt, so that's what he wants to throw.
And, sure, this is a story of loss, as bored as any other, but it's a story,

as well, of the implausible, of men who'll name their loss in a hatred for
gooks, investing in chance and misfortune to find their idea of home
little more than a legion hall littered with oaktag and the swish of a janitor's

broom. Can you hear it? Can you see it hold in the air like a lazy pop fly?
The infield grass, the smell of rain? Seven years from marrying my mother
in a simple ceremony, in a church on Euclid Avenue, and seven years

from the frail idea of children, my father's elbow is about to snap.

2.

Forsythia climbs the fence in a lot at Le Cordon Bleu, and the Interboro
    reminds no one of the sea.

Do you, Miriam, take this man to be your husband? Do you promise to
    love and no one answer, will you promise?

Will you make of your heart an empire in the slow coming-out of sleep,
    will you make of this world

an elegy? It's an old mistake, but you are young. The Gem shuts its doors
    to the Jew, our histories marked

in band shells, in Meyers luncheonette, Saint Anthony's sleeved in dust.
    In brownfields, affordable housing,

in churchyards and trestles, from Fulton to Rockaway, Emanuel Church
    of Christ. And you, James,

do you take this woman to be your bride? Do you promise to love and no
    one answer, will you promise?

Will you make of your love, will you make of this world? Will you make
    of your heart an empire

3.

of men who move dimly, and the city that never was. And Joan Didion, come
out of the west for the first time. Come out of the west for the Biltmore clock,
for Madison Ave. and a slight rain. For the Lever House and Lester Lanin on
the tip of a cabdriver's tongue, for Diana Vreeland, Hattie Carnegie, for Irving
Penn's Deardorff lens in a studio on Fifth Ave., the north windows streaked
with exhaust. Come out of the west for the Brooklyn Bridge, for a hint of lilac
and jasmine soap, "I've Got a Crush On You," and getting an eyeful of *the
wastes of Queens,* the wrought *valley of ash.*

It takes a worried man to sing a worried song
I'm worried now, but I won't be worried long

And Saul Bellow in a Chester Barrie suit, daydreaming the hemline of a Queens
College adjunct as he conjures Madeleine Pontritter, Herzog's second ex-
wife, brought into the church by an atavist and sacred albs, who wants now
only *to live in one of those streets of brick, semi-detached parochial houses in the
dull wilderness of Queens borough,* hidebound Madeleine *fussing over Communion
dresses, with a steady Irish husband who sweeps up crumbs at the biscuit factory.*
And the borough written from the armrest of a wing chair housed in the
Smithsonian, from Norman Lear's mouthpiece, taped before a live studio
audience, Carroll O'Connor in syndicated light.

It takes a worried man to sing a worried song
I'm worried now, but I won't be worried long

And *the New York Times,* discover Rockaway for a season, *the sliver of dilapidated
bungalows, drug-riddled public housing and W.P.A.-era boardwalk at the end point of
the A train,* and the New Rockaway Arcade, abandoned "Coming Soon." I need
a sideline. I need to hear it so plain the entire gym understands, what even my
mother can't ignore. *Get into the teeth or sit next to me.* My mother's first car was
a Dodge Plymouth. She buys it used for $600 from a dealer on Knickerbocker
Ave. She has saved for three years. She is twenty-two years old.

The devil wears a hypocrite shoe

She teaches sixth grade math at P.S. 45. On Schaefer and Evergreen. It's 1967. The faculty chipped in to buy a spare car battery in case of emergency. They keep it in a sink closet. Tonight, my mother leaves the building at 7:30, and walks to her car. Walks past the brownstones on Bushwick Avenue. Past Woolworth's. She turns the key in the ignition, and the car whines. *Come on,* she says. *Start,* she says. She turns the key again. She thinks of calling her father, then of the spare battery in the sink closet. She gets out of the car and opens the hood.

The devil wears a hypocrite shoe

Her father is a pressman for the *New York Post*. He works nights locking cast-metal plates into a rotary. In a high-ceilinged room overlooking vacant lots. His hair is thick, lightly graying, and his back is still supple. Over dinner, his daughter explains to him how someone must have stolen the battery *long after the kids were dismissed.* The next morning, he follows her to work. *You can replace the battery tomorrow,* he says. He parks behind her car on Halsey. And as she explains the times tables to the children of Bushwick, he sits on the hood with a baseball bat, so that *no spook touches this car again.*

The devil wears a hypocrite shoe
And if you don't watch he'll slip it on you

There's no hiding place

4.

down here, so the reception is held in Whitman's tense,
unfolding, still possible, the maid of honor reapplies
lipstick before a bathroom mirror and worries over her
toast, the cook slices potatoes, absent-minded, beside
a boiling pot, the best man, a boy really, orders a shot
of whiskey, then raises his glass to the bride and groom
(in less than a year, on a trail north of Hue an hour past
midnight, two bullets will tear through his chest like a saw
to cut him down; he is holding his breath, he will share
the earth with emperors), the spinning-girl twirls her skirt
around, the young mother watches intently, afraid at how
much love she feels, the band finishes their pre-dinner set,
loud as a football team, the bride's father cuts into his steak,
the fat pools in his plate, the bartender, asleep on his feet,
tops a highball glass of scotch and ice with club soda, he
doesn't like the work, but he's lucky for it, after high school,
and after the draft brought him home 4-A, service completed,
a chaplain's assistant at Fort Polk, Louisiana, or, like the groom,
the only son of a single mother making less than minimum
wage (*we'll get by without him,* my grandmother told the
draft board, her pride outpacing any deferment), he took a job
loading mail trucks at the airport and was let go in cut backs,
but now the wait staff begins to clear the tables of half-eaten
cake, the parish priest smokes a last cigarette, and the groom
traces the slope of his new bride's hand as the best man, three
sheets to the wind, sings "Two Hearts Are Better than One,"
in a pitch as strained as "Those Were the Days."

THE TENANT OF FIRE:
a sequence

1. HAWK-MAN

I'm a man who believed that I died
twenty years ago, and I live like a man
who is dead already.

Malcolm X

The still eyes of Malcolm X, stilled by an f-stop and shutter.
Winter, 1965. Malcolm is leaving a car, gelatin-silver print,
portrait of a tenant of fire. He stares into the camera

like a performer breaking scene, the sureness of his death
the missive I read this morning after another chapter
from Marable's best-selling biography, bookended

by Malcolm's Pan-Africanism and the firebombing
of his East Elmhurst home. I don't have to read further;
I know of the week to come—the flight to Detroit,

the Ford Auditorium, the interview where he'll name his time
a time for martyrs. I know of the Audubon and the smell
of smoke, folding chairs littered like leaflets across the ballroom

floor. I've heard who and why as you've heard who and why,
and that if it wasn't them it was surely someone else,
so I've left the book open to the insert, Malcolm in a black

fez, dark suit, Malcolm getting out of an Oldsmobile.
The image is editorial, a day after the fire, but the composition
is classical: *The Deposition*, Christ's descent from the cross.

Two policemen flank the stoop like the Virgin and St. John,
framing the martyr in motion. Or like guards at a national gallery,
security for the fire. Malcolm's body is bent; he can rise

or collapse, taut as a spring. His *hawk-man's eyes* seem
hollowed out; the horn-rimmed glasses like the lip of a well
at the center of an emptying town where the townspeople

have left behind furniture in the street, an end table
and lampshade, a wingchair no longer worth its weight.
An upturned couch at the foot of an elm. And beside

the wintering tree, in gradations of gray but for the blacked-
out windows and an awning nearly paper white, the single-
family house bought by the Nation of Islam in 1959.

Fire as eviction. Fire as the shape of history.
23-11 97th Street. I was twelve when I first saw it,
the iconic brick long obscured by aluminum siding the color

of public swimming pools. It was summer. A shy kid,
I could go days without lifting my eyes, but on the court
I burned like a blockbuster, crowding you from baseline

to baseline. So after a game at Elmcor—a loss, I think—
our coach, a grave man with a voice that always thinned
by the fourth quarter, gathered us on the boulevard

and took us all to *Brother Malcolm's house*. That's how
he said it, in a low rasp, *Brother Malcolm*, as if
on speaking terms, as if family. I didn't know what for.

To me the name alone was dangerous, a mark
on someone else's map. A past and a threat. I couldn't know
in a few years we'd sweat Olaf's, Xs grown ubiquitous

as Starter jackets, Denzel playing hero to the men
on 42nd Street who called out *white devil* when my father
passed; the threat turning profit, packaged and sold.

I was three trains from home, Coach walking us
through the side streets of Corona. *The neighborhood
built this airport,* he said, pointing to a control tower

from the corner of Malcolm's block. *Grandfathers. Great uncles.*
Not mine. My grandfather came here from Belfast,
the youngest of five boys, and built a life in Brooklyn,

two daughters, a son, and carried with him a thirst
that sent him out of the house, through a series of odd jobs—
midnight security at the Navy yard, singing waiter

at The Welcome Inn—to a second family,
until he found himself washing the hardwood floors
at Blessed Sacrament Elementary. All around him

book reports pinned to bulletins framed in lacquered oak—
*The Clue of the Leaning Chimney, The Secret of the Wooden
Lady*—and math tests stamped *Great Work!* Outside,

it was fall; the noon shadows slowly folding back
into themselves. He held a mop above the wringer.
He was still. And the more I write the more still

he becomes, another Daphne, transformed from flesh
to idea, forever rooted in the same place.
That's the problem. I can't conjure him out of that hallway.

I can't find a place for him here. Not in Corona in 1989.
Or East Elmhurst in 2017, where my wife and I crouch
to greet a pair of tabbies parading the tree-lined street.

No monument marks the home of Malcolm X,
but *People would come here all the time,* Mrs. Mack tells us,
hurrying the cats, Biggie and Petite, into her front yard

with a broom. *Muslims. White people. But it's different now,*
she says. *The neighborhood's changed. Farrakhan used to come
all the time. He'd block the street; his men taking pictures.*

Those boys would brush his suit when he got out of the car.
Give me a break! she adds with a wry smile. A yellow cab
idles in front of a neighbor's house. The cats idle, too.

Last week my girlfriend said to me, 'You never told me
you lived across from Malcolm's house,' and I said to her,
'I thought you already knew.'

2. GOODBYE, PICCADILLY

"I am the woman in this house. None other."

Toni Morrison

In its place a Marriott Marquis the width of Broadway.
Poured concrete, beveled siding, brown glass flanking
a twenty-four-hour parking garage. Nineteen hundred

air-conditioned rooms complete with coffee makers,
thirty-two-inch flat-screen TVs, and movies on demand.
A multilingual staff stands by to assist with dry cleaning.

When the Piccadilly closed, Mrs. Mack picked up work
at the Drake, then the Waldorf. *All those years on my feet,*
she said, n*ow a half hour's thirty minutes too long.* She eyed

the fruit salad we'd brought, still in its Tupperware,
then me. *Next time just bring something for the cats.*
It was late spring; a rose bush bloomed along

the fenced-in lot where someone had left a carousel horse
propped like a Santa Claus among the ragweed.
We sat out on her stoop, the two of us and Mrs. Mack,

talking about the airport noise, about Malcolm's house
across the street and the tenants who live there still—
the old man who couldn't leave his bed, the daughter

who should have held the service in the neighborhood.
Her son bought the house next door, Mrs. Mack said.
It should have been here. I asked again about Guyana

and the view of the Atlantic along the Sea Wall,
but then a young girl, no more than ten, with twists in her hair,
stopped stone-still in front of the low gate that marked

Mrs. Mack's walkway as if caught in a game
of freeze tag, and sang out in her soft voice, *Hello, Mrs. Mack*,
then lowered her eyes. *I see you, Crystal*,

Mrs. Mack answered. *Tell your mom I see you. Go on*,
and the girl ran off. And there's so much I don't know,
so much more, so let me be quiet a moment,

let someone else speak. *I came to the U.S. through
the agency. It was two years before I could leave,
the queues went out the door. All these women!*

*I got my greencard, here, at the airport. Then I flew
to Baltimore, for a family in Glenn Dale.
Their house overlooked the farm. Corn in one season,*

*string beans the next. I took care of their boy, a smart boy,
whip smart, beautiful. He had blue eyes like yours,
fine blond hair. His mother, she had a condition.*

*She couldn't hold him. She had to lie in bed
with a machine that made her muscles work.
These white people don't know how to raise a boy.*

I'm sorry, she said to me, but not to my wife.
*I had to teach him how to stop wetting the bed.
I carried him into the bathroom after he fell asleep,*

*sat him down on the toilet, and turned on the water
until he peed. Every night.* Stratified reproduction,
we might think; the idea that a mother's labor

unspools like a film, determined by race and ethnicity,
gender and migration; that the work itself casts out like a net
to grandchildren, great-grandchildren, nieces and nephews,

a communal foster care, but the mythic America
is my own blond boyhood, battered sneakers and uniforms,
and mile after mile of cut grass across the country.

We haven't been back to see Mrs. Mack since her grandson's
graduation. She said she'd stopped taking her insulin,
that her legs were worse each day. I said we'd be gone

until next spring, that I'd call from California.
I tried once, but she was too tired to talk. Lately,
I've been thinking of that young boy, of Clifford—

I hadn't told you his name—who must be my age by now,
who inherited his father's estate and still dreams of wind
at the edge of a sea. And I'm sure of my part in this story;

I know I'd be the fine hairs of that beautiful boy
and never the hand that strokes them. And I'm afraid.
I'm afraid I might not see her again. After Glenn Dale,

Mrs. Mack moved in with her half-brother in Jamaica, Queens,
and started working the laundry rooms in those midtown
hotels, the Drake being her favorite—its stone façade,

the cherry trees in bloom. *Presidents stayed at the Waldorf,*
she told me. *The Clintons, Obama. But not this one, no.*
He's got his own to sleep in.

3. THE CURTAIN

Sometimes whole days slipped past without my noticing . . .

Larry Levis

My youth? I can't hear it anywhere, Larry.
Not in the whippoorwill's call at Jamaica Bay;
not in a Clinton Hill townhouse, single bedrooms available,

$1850/month. No. For a while I was the only white boy
on the team. Then I wasn't. In Delaware, they thought
Puerto Rican. In Virginia, *light skinned.* That these men

could mistake a tight fade for Spanish Harlem, mistook
a handle for code, as if context were the only determinant.
Ryan? Shammgod joked. *Motherfucker's grandfather*

still try to own us. When I was fifteen, Spike Lee brought
fifty of the city's top high-school players to Clinton Hill
for a 40 Acres and a Mule clinic: three meals a day,

SAT prep, and a week of guest lectures on black masculinity.
At Pratt Institute. We slept in the dorms. At night
we hopped the fence, bought 40s at the bodega on DeKalb.

The best players, the sure things, slept in in the morning,
then busted my ass in the afternoon. I couldn't check them;
couldn't keep them in front. Steph and Rafer. Kareem Reid.

Too much. And the lectures? I remember Spike's.
About money and black bodies, and what a college makes
off your labor, your talent. You. *A plantation mentality,*

he said, ahead of Walter Byers, executive director
and architect of the NCAA, who'd name it the same,
resurrected and blessed. I sat cross-legged in front

of Spike, in my free jersey and sneakers, and a pair
of Riverside shorts, the golden hawk like a bankroll,
access and all I'd ever want. For years Riverside Church

was AAU basketball, rivaled only by the Gauchos
in the Bronx or the New Jersey Roadrunners.
Before Kenny Anderson lit up Bobby Hurley at Georgia Tech,

he lit him up for the Church at Columbia.
And that image, that icon, the ball clutched in its talons,
meant more to us than the scholarships to come.

DI. DII. It didn't matter. You wear the Church once,
you own it. You signify. We got our first pair
of free sneakers after a Citywide game at Gauchos gym.

Adidas. From Sonny Vaccaro. We were sold;
we played Bitch for the extras. Sonny's name rang out
in the Bronx, in Brooklyn and Queens. Uptown. Wherever.

A Calabrese from Western Pennsylvania, he founded
the Dapper Dan Roundball Classic in '65, and the invitation-only
ABCD camp where All-Americans built their brand.

Sonny was inexorable, like the men in suits—the *abonnés*—
sequestered to the edges of Degas's frame, patrons
of *a world of pink and white*. The *abonnés* kept to the wings,

to the foyers and rehearsal rooms of the Palais Garnier,
selecting their favorites—the girls who bloomed
in the footlights—with a curator's care,

but in *Le rideau* the *abonnés* stalk the canvas,
obscured by stage flats or in plain sight, their dark suits,
their backs turned, cutouts in the dressing. The dancers

are not the point here, the machines of their bodies
reduced to rose beneath a curtain, save for one
in the corner, beribboned, fleeing the decor.

The dance instills in you something that sets you apart,
Degas would write, himself an *abonné*. *One knows*
that in your world / Queens are made of distance

and greasepaint. Of plumb lines and gutter sylphs.
Of a sponsor's foresight, bodies long and lithe as Steph's
or Kareem's. Shammgod was broad shouldered,

legs like goalposts. A McDonald's All American,
if you kept him in front he went right through you.
He had this crossover like a rope trick. He'd toss the ball

out from his hip as if losing control, then change direction,
pulling it back across his body with his off hand
like opening a curtain. You can google it. I'll wait . . .

Once, in Myrtle Beach, Shammgod broke out for thirty
in the second half against a team from Florida, then broke
into their hotel and stole all their sneakers.

The tournament caught word, but Shammgod already threw
the bag off a bridge on the side of a road. The troopers
had to let us go. Shammgod just smiled, a Band-Aid

under his right eye like a family coat of arms.
Shammgod Wells, broad-shouldered son of God the father.
Not Steph or Skip, Boogie or Kareem. The only handle,

God Shammgod.

4. DUKE ELLINGTON, LIVE AT THE AQUACADE

*Fate's being kind to me. It doesn't want me
to be too famous too young.*

Duke Ellington

A paycheck. A nadir. Hired as accompaniment
for sequined swimmers in an amphitheater in Queens.
To keep the band working. A footnote.

I was born at Newport in '56, Ellington was fond
of saying. Born again, to be fair, ushered
by Paul Gonsalves's twenty-seven chorus solo

and a white woman's dance. Born aloft a tritone,
tethered to the breath of the thirty-six-year-old's
tenor sax. Though just months earlier,

Sir Duke was made to descend to the speckled stage
of the Aquacade, in the heart of Queens. For six weeks,
Ellington and his orchestra—minus Gonsalves

and Willie Cook, minus Rick Henderson, Dave Black,
and Britt Woodman, each replaced by members
of the Local 802—played medleys behind a forty-foot

screen of water. "Mood Indigo" bleeding into "Solitude,"
"The Mooche" giving over to "Perdido,"
then "Take the 'A' Train," a rose to the stitching

of Bed-Stuy to Harlem, to black modernity.
Picture it: the nearly all-white crowd, working men
and wives, their sons and daughters, cheering

every lift and gasping at the fireworks filling
the night sky. 1955. A boy shifts in his seat.
His eyes dart from the divers to the dancing waves

pink as cotton candy. His mind wanders.
And Ellington, tired and aloof, pushes his way
through an old arrangement of "Sophisticated

Lady." He won't return for a second set, excused
while another conductor leads the band
augmented by strings. *To hell with it,*

Ellington mutters, lighting another cigarette
in his dressing room, Newport still an undiscovered country.
America's Debussy, alone, unaccustomed,

wiping the sweat from his forehead with an embroidered
handkerchief, four miles and four years
from the East Elmhurst home of Malcolm X.

Here are the relics of our future. Here is the future
of us all, the new face of a nation. *In thirty years,*
a museum guide tells us, *students today, their children*

will be the first generation raised in the U.S.,
we nod our approval, his smile blooming,
where white is no longer the majority, as it hasn't been

here in Queens since the nineties.
The dancing woman was Elaine Anderson,
a thirty-three year old socialite, her image printed

on the back jacket of the Columbia LP—
The gal who launched 7,000 cheers. Whose father
was made rich by a shipwreck. Ellington's Helen

in a cocktail dress, platinum-blonde bringer
of glad news, who danced in ecstasy
as the cameras turned away from the stage to find her.

They tell me I saved the night for the Ellington band.
It's how you look at it, she said, her memory
held like a clutch. *The glass was half-filled—I caused it.*

Half-empty—Gonsalves did.

5. NOTHING BEATS A FAIR

As long as you're on the side of parks, you're on the side of the angels.

Robert Moses

Everything but the ice was carpeted—
the flight of stairs, benches and columns.
Carpet climbing the walls, stapled to plywood,

the sort bought by the roll, promising too many years,
too much of a discount. I'd look down from above
the scratched glass, the bad ice once home

to the General Assembly of the UN, where men
in neckties voted the partitioning of Palestine;
it was a skating rink before that, a skating rink again.

But the space still held the feel of what shouldn't last.
In 1964 a pavilion for Robert Moses's World's Fair
advertising "Peace Through Understanding,"

as though outpacing the Soviets in equanimity.
Walt Disney sold Mustangs and Pepsi-Cola
with animatronics and a twelve-minute boat ride

espousing interracial accord. Warhol showed the city
an image of itself: a twenty- by twenty-foot silkscreen:
mug shots, our *13 Most Wanted Men.*

My mother served Löwenbräu at the beer garden.
Seventeen, she wore a French braid, a cotton dress,
and an apron at work. I imagine her train ride,

East New York to Flushing Meadows-Corona Park,
her transfer at Sutphin, then again at Roosevelt,
a bead of sweat starting at the hairline.

Or does she drive in with Roseanne,
someone with a real license and a used car?
I haven't promised a thing to the muses;

I can go on not knowing, so that on a Sunday
in August, my mother can leave for work an hour early,
after Mass. She can wear an A-line skirt, a gray plaid,

white blouse and stockings, black shoes pinched
at the toes. She comes to see Michelangelo's *Pietà*,
the jewel of Moses's fair, before her shift begins.

To keep the lines moving, and to keep the Madonna
and Christ at some remove, the pavilion erected
bulletproof glass and three motorized walkways

positioned at differing heights. She hasn't met
my father yet. She's seventeen. And what she'll remember
of the great sculpture—on loan from the Basilica of Saint Peter,

brought across the dark Atlantic, lashed with steel
to a liner's deck—what she'll recall is not
the blameless face of Mary, even younger than her own face,

or the pulses and veins of Christ's body so finely
wrought, but the lighting. The votive lights.
Cold. Directed. *Like an aquarium*, she tells me.

How fish seem so otherworldly in that blue light.
As it turned out, my mother never saw the *Pietà*,
and no one ever saw Warhol's silkscreen, no one

but the men who called for its removal.
Governor Rockefeller ordered the *13 Most Wanted Men*—
seven were Italian-American—be replaced immediately,

though the accused would remain, their *cauliflower ears,*
their scarred faces, specters behind a thin coat
of aluminum silver. *It's more me now,*

Warhol would say, staring up at the monochrome block
one year later. One year later the fair closed at a loss.
The New York Pavilion would go on unemployed

for the rest of the century, rusting alongside
the Grand Central, until given over to a memory
of winter, to Eddie Brown, the New York Stars

vs. the Green Machine. Eddie came from the Bronx.
He skated stiff-legged, upright. He was the only black kid
on the ice. *Blacker than the puck,* he'd say

to my brother on road trips. He was sixteen,
played left wing for the Stars, scored three goals
in two years. I was there for one.

A home game. I don't remember the goal,
a wrist shot or a redirect, a rebound chipped in at the crease.
I don't remember the period, the score, or much else

but the man who turned away from the ice
and to no one in particular said, *They let that nigger score.*
I was ten. I thought I knew who he meant;

the boys who carried box cutters on the J train,
who'd slash your face for nothing.
The ones my mother loved, in her school,

with razors under their tongues. The punch lines, setups—
So Al Sharpton, Jesse Jackson, and Farrakhan
are brought to Rome to meet the Pope.

The boys who stole Frankie's bike outside of Lane.
Fucked him up, too. My father just leaned into the railing,
his back hunched like a goalie's. He didn't flinch.

He kept his eye on the ice, on his son jumping the boards,
lining up for the face-off. My mother stepped back,
then seemed to harden like the women in those stories,

in *D'aulaires' Book of Greek Myths,* who were
transformed because they would not give consent.
No one said a thing. No one answered. No one dared

question the man or the silence that wished
to make plain again the arena lights. An awful silence.
Tender. And easy to forget.

6. A GUN TO THE HEART OF THE CITY

I was in New York City for the stall-in. Got there early that morning, was walking through Harlem, and right next to a filling station, a cat walked up to me and said, "Hey baby, can you loan me three pennies? I want to buy some gas. I'm driving to the World's Fair."

Dick Gregory

Eighteen hundred drivers volunteered. Eighteen hundred
cars to merge onto the Grand Central Parkway,
their noses pointed toward the World's Fair in Queens,

their gas tanks near empty. Eighteen hundred men
and women for police reform and school integration,
for fair housing, inclusive labor, for the letter of the law.

A Crown Victorian sputters eastbound along the L.I.E.
An Impala stalls the Van Wyck at Hillside—
a missing inhibitor. Two sedans, discarded near Flatbush,

are *put on display*. It's morning, April 22, 1964.
A friend misremembers. And in his misremembering
my mother sits in traffic. Clenched jaw, brake lights,

the car hoods slick with rain. It's her first day
at the Löwenbräu Gardens. She's running late.
But the *New York Journal-American*

had already declaimed the stall-in, first proposed
by Louis Lomax in a speech at Queens College,
as *a clear threat to law and order*. The *Post* called it

merely *sound and fury, carrying no clear message*.
Eighteen hundred cars *on exhibit*. Eighteen hundred extras
playing themselves. In his study, Lomax

must have thought back to Valdosta, Georgia,
his days as a shoeshine boy in an all-white barbershop,
how the laughter always doubled when the owner,

a garrulous man, would duck-walk across the checkered
floor to demonstrate how best to make your way
through a lynch crowd. To be up close.

The night before the Fair opened, Mayor Wagner,
a liberal Democrat, denounced the would-be stall-in,
naming it *a gun to the heart of the city.*

Metaphor. Metonymy. The crime reported in advance.
Michael Brown *bulking up to run through the shots.*
It's three a.m. and your children are safe.

What did you think would happen? A demonstration?
A riot? The city deployed over one thousand patrolmen
to the highways of Brooklyn and Queens.

Twenty-three protestors were arrested
in Jackson Heights, but the Grand Central was clear,
and Robert Moses welcomed fifty thousand visitors

to his *World of Tomorrow.* In another version,
one swept clean of our figurations, the metaphors
meant to mug us in the dark, my mother sits in traffic

on the Interboro Parkway, her mind a punch clock.
All around her the graves of artists and abolitionists—
Thomas Downing, Arturo Schomburg, James McCune Smith.

Car horns blare and bleat their discontent. My mother
lights a cigarette. She fidgets. One mile ahead
a woman has turned herself into a conceit,

blocking traffic with a stalled Chrysler; her placard,
Discrimination Is a Wall Which Side Are You On?
And the fat policemen who arrive in a huff,

and the tow trucks' blinking lights,
and no one to spy the *World of Tomorrow,*
no one to walk through its gates.

NOTES

The book's first epigraph is taken from Leslie Fiedler's "Come Back to the Raft Ag'in, Huck Honey!" The second epigraph is taken from the traditional American song "There's No Hiding Place Down Here."

"Not Once" quotes from John Keats's "La Belle Dame Sans Merci."

"The Rise of the Colored Empires" quotes from F. Scott Fitzgerald's *The Great Gatsby*, John Jeremiah Sullivan's August 23, 2012, *New York Times* article "Venus and Serena Against the World," and Barbara Will's essay *"The Great Gatsby* and the Obscene Word."

"The Brigadier and the Golf Widow" quotes from Jack Gilbert's "Finding Something."

The song quoted in "This Is Cinerama" is Muddy Waters's "You Can't Lose What You Ain't Never Had."

"Compensation" quotes from Ralph Waldo Emerson's essay of the same title. The song quoted is Fugees's "Ready or Not."

"At Broad Channel" is indebted to Polly Murray's memoir *The Widening Circle: A Lyme Disease Pioneer Tells Her Story*. The "young artist" mentioned in the poem is Vincent van Gogh.

"At Steepletop" is indebted to Nancy Milford's *Savage Beauty: The Life of Edna St. Vincent Millay*.

"On the Cooling Board" quotes from John Berryman's "Dream Song 3: A Stimulant for an Old Beast."

"Why Bother?" quotes from Jonathan Franzen's essay "Perchance to Dream: In the Age of Images, a Reason to Write Novels," which appeared in the April 1996 issue of *Harper's* and was later reprinted in the collection *How to Be Alone*, under the title "Why Bother?" The poem also quotes from Friedrich

Nietzsche's essay "On Truth and Lying in an Extra-Moral Sense," translated by David J. Parent.

"Via Negativa" quotes from Robert Lowell's "For George Santayana."

"Ommie Wise" quotes from John Berryman's "Dream Song 29."

"The Conjurer" adapts a line from Steve Gehrke's "Capitalism," and quotes from Jack Gilbert's "Finding Something." For the story of Houdini's performance in Australia, I am indebted to Ruth Brandon's *The Life and Many Deaths of Harry Houdini*.

"In the Pines" quotes from Alice Notley's "In the Pines."

"Motherless Children" quotes from Walt Whitman's "Song of Myself."

"4-A": The first section opens with a quote from Jorie Graham's "Untitled." Section 3 quotes from F. Scott Fitzgerald's *The Great Gatsby*, Joan Didion's "Goodbye to All That," the traditional American song "Worried Man Blues," Saul Bellow's *Herzog*, the June 15, 2011, *New York Times* article "Taking the A Train to Summer," and the traditional American song "There's No Hiding Place Down Here."

"Hawk-Man": The epigraph is from a statement by Malcolm X late in his life, regarding the Nation of Islam. The poem quotes from Gwendolyn Brooks's "Malcolm X."

"Goodbye, Piccadilly": The epigraph is from Toni Morrison's *Tar Baby*. The theory of "stratified reproduction" was first introduced by Shellee Colen in "'With Respect and Feelings': Voices of West Indian Child Care Workers in New York City."

"The Curtain": The epigraph is from Larry Levis's "The Poet at Seventeen." The poem quotes from Walter Byers's *Unsportsmanlike Conduct: Exploiting College Athletes*.

"Duke Ellington, Live at the Aquacade": The epigraph is from Duke Ellington's response to the removal of his name from consideration for the 1965 Pulitzer Prize for Music. The poem quotes from and is indebted to John Fass Morton's *Backstory in Blue: Ellington at Newport '56*, as well as John Edward Hasse's *Beyond Category: The Life and Genius of Duke Ellington*. The poem also adopts the title of Roger Sanjek's anthropological study of Elmhurst and Corona, *The Future of Us All: Race and Neighborhood Politics in New York City*.

"Nothing Beats a Fair": The epigraph, attributed to Robert Moses, is from Robert Caro's *The Power Broker: Robert Moses and the Fall of New York*. The poem is indebted to Joseph Tirella's *Tomorrow-Land: The 1964–65 World's Fair and the Transformation of America*.

"A Gun to the Heart of the City": The epigraph is from a 1964 comedy routine performed by Dick Gregory. The poem is indebted to Brian Purnell's *Fighting Jim Crow in the County of Kings: The Congress of Racial Equity in Brooklyn*. The poem quotes from officer Darren Wilson's grand jury testimony on the 2014 killing of Michael Brown, as well as from a 2008 Hillary Clinton presidential primary television advertisement. For the story of Louis Lomax in Valdosta, Georgia, I am indebted to Lomax's *The Negro Revolt*.

ACKNOWLEDGMENTS

Thanks to the editors and journals where these poems previously appeared:

"Not Once" appeared in *CURA: A Literary Magazine of Art & Action*; "The Rise of the Colored Empires" appeared in *Tupelo Quarterly*; "The Brigadier and the Golf Widow" appeared in *The Journal*; "This Is Cinerama" appeared in *Ploughshares*; "Home by the Sea" appeared in *Southern Humanities Review*; "Skip to My Lou" appeared in the *James Franco Review*; "Compensation" appeared in *Ninth Letter*; "At Broad Channel" and "Why Bother?" appeared in *AGNI Online*; "At Steepletop" appeared in *The Literary Review*; "When the World's on Fire" appeared in *Killer Verse: Poems about Murder and Mayhem*; "On the Cooling Board" appeared in *HIV Here & Now*; "Via Negativa" appeared in *LUNA*; "The Lemon Ice King" appeared in *The Saint Ann's Review*; "Stagger Lee" appeared in *Grist*; "The Conjurer," "The Curtain," and "Nothing Beats a Fair" appeared in the *Southern Review*; "In the Pines" appeared in the *Blueshift Journal*; "Motherless Children" and "4-A" appeared in *Newtown Literary*; "Hawk-Man" and "Duke Ellington, Live at the Aquacade" appeared in *Virginia Quarterly Review*; "Goodbye, Piccadilly" and "A Gun to the Heart of the City" appeared in *Blackbird*.

"An Offering of Steam" appeared as a limited-edition, letterpressed broadside from the Center for Book Arts, New York, New York.

Some of the poems in this book appear in *Death of a Nativist*, winner of the 2016 Poetry Society of America National Chapbook Fellowship, selected by Linda Gregerson.

Thank you:

To my family and friends. To my brothers, Jason and Matthew, for always looking out. To Kristine, Vicky, and Thomas, for your love and support. To Lauren, James, and Simone, for lighting the way ahead. To Aunt Kathy, Aunt Patricia, Aunt Rosalie, Uncle Bob, and Uncle Mickey, for lighting the way back. To my father-in-law, Kwork Lun Lin, in loving memory. To Jimmy, Jill, Michael, Nancy, Kelly, Bill, Tony, Kassidy, Allyson, Kate, and Emily, for all that we share. To Bobby, with us always. To Peter, Phil, Vinny, Dana, Leandra, Georgia, Grace, and Steve, for my luck to share this with you. To Cenza, Angelina, Vin, Lucy, Ellie, Zoe, Stevie, Tommy, and Riley, for the haunted houses. To Mr. Venza, Mrs. Venza, Mr. Navetta, Ms. Kathy, Mr. Pete, Mr. Savino, Marie, and Frank, for your care over so many years. In memory of my father, James Black. I miss you always. For my mother, Miriam Black, the most remarkable person I know. I can never thank you enough.

To my first teachers, Kimiko Hahn and John Weir, for giving me this life.

To Ciaran Berry and Aracelis Girmay, for your kindness and example. For showing me how it's done.

To the writers whose insights helped shape these poems, especially Aaron Balkan, Nellie Bridge, Nicole Cooley, Miles Grier, Caroline Hong, Diana Khoi Nguyen, Sameer Pandya, Greg Pardlo, and Noel Sikorski.

To my teachers and mentors, especially B. H. Fairchild, Eamon Grennan, Melissa Hammerle, Marie Howe, Phillis Levin, Marilyn Nelson, and Tom Sleigh. In memory of Phil Levine. It was my good fortune to be one of your students.

To my friends and classmates in the Creative Writing Program at NYU. I'm still learning from you all these years later.

To Alice Quinn and the Poetry Society of America, for supporting my work with a PSA Chapbook Fellowship.

To Linda Gregerson, for selecting *Death of a Nativist*.

To my friends and colleagues at Queens College/CUNY. To Ashna Ali, Ala Alryyes, Mindy Altman, Sara Alvarez, Jamie Arizmendy, Barbara Bowen, June Bobb, Iemanjá Brown, Fred Buell, Glenn Burger, Jeff Cassvan, Scott Cheshire, Seo-Young Chu, Joe Cuomo, Basuli Deb, Annmarie Drury, Hugh English, Duncan Faherty, Beverly Fenig-Ducat, Kevin Ferguson, Gloria Fisk, Tom Frosch,

Fred Gardaphe, Sue Goldhaber, Marci Goodman, Hillary Gulley, Carrie Hintz, Robin Hizme, Briallen Hopper, Naomi Jackson, Ahktar Khan, Steve Kruger, Eunjeong Lee, Natalie Léger, Cliff Mak, Rich Marotta, Rich McCoy, Maaza Mengiste, Alexandra Meriç, Hillary Miller, Wayne Moreland, Marco Navarro, Uche Nduka, Tony O'Brien, Bill Orchard, Megan Paslawski, John Rice, David Richter, Michael Sargent, Talia Schaffer, Veronica Schanoes, Harold Schechter, Richard Schotter, Roger Sedarat, Kate Schnur, Beth Sherman, Sian Silyn Roberts, Heather Simon, Rhoda Sirlin, Kim Smith, Tiffany Smith, Tiffany Thomas, Jason Tougaw, Amy Tucker, John Tytell, Andrea Walkden, Amy Wan, John Wang, Gordon Whatley, Bette Weidman, Karen Weingarten, Chastity Whitaker, Chris Williams, and Evan Zimroth, for fostering such a supportive community at Queens College.

To my students, who I learn from all the time.

To Tommy Helm and everyone at Empire Studio, for your art and friendship.

To the institutions that have supported the writing of these poems. To the Adirondack Center for Writing, the Millay Colony for the Arts, PLAYA, the Sewanee Writers' Conference, the T. S. Eliot House, and the Queens Council on the Arts.

To everyone at the University of Pittsburgh Press. To Ed Ochester, for believing in this manuscript. To Maria Sticco, Chloe Wertz, and Alex Wolfe, for your tireless work. To Joel W. Coggins, for your beautiful design.

Finally, to Esther, my partner in everything. Every poem. Every line. Thank you for sharing this life with me.